Dragon Slayers

A Story of Conquering Change

By Gail Lindsay

Dragon Slayer – A Story of Conquering Change
ISBN 9781489510228

Dragon slayer silhouette graphic by Grz Maaike
Cover design by Rita Toews

Drop By for a Visit to our Website at www.dragonslayerleader.com

Many thanks to my husband Kent and my family and friends for their support and enthusiasm for Dragon Slaying. This book is truly a labor of love and passion for leadership. Change is never easy, but the results are miraculous and well worth the effort. Don't let dragons stand in the way of your dreams, goals, and what you know in your heart to be right and true.

Table of Contents

Introduction   Page 1

The Valley Of Good Enough   Page 6

The Land of Progress   Page 45

Dragon Slayer's Key to Leading Change   Page 50

Dragon Slayer's Change Checklist   Page 52

Qualities of a Dragon Slayer   Page 53

Qualities of a Dragon   Page 54

Dragon Slayers and Armor   Page 55

Dragons   Page 58

Heroes   Page 65

DRAGON SLAYERS

The road to change often seems dark and difficult to navigate, but once started it gets easier.

Introduction

When you stop to consider the attributes of great leadership, one that tops the list is the ability to influence and lead change. Leadership does not reside in an individual, but rather it is the result of a dynamic influence relationship. It requires more than simply navigating barriers to change. Leadership, at its best, is an artful masterpiece of passion (heart), wisdom (mind), valor (spirit), and strength.

Passion is an intense, enthusiastic devotion to a cause. It requires tireless diligence, supernatural energy, and long-term commitment. Passion is conviction harnessed to be a driving force.

Wisdom is a deep understanding of people, events, or situations that results in the ability to apply perceptions and judgments. It requires control of your emotions to allow the comprehension of what is true to be coupled with optimum judgment as to action.

Valor is courage in the defense of a noble cause. It is the ability to encounter danger with firmness and personal bravery. It requires determination, boldness, and a spirit to face danger without fear.

Strength is the inherent capacity to manifest energy and to endure. It is the ability to withstand great force or stress. It requires self-assurance, mental skills, and the physical capability to confront difficulties of all kinds.

Too often in organizations, change is implemented as a strategy or a means to an end, rather than as an opportunity to develop and strengthen relationships and enhance the fabric of culture. As a result, change becomes a negative experience that divides, rather than being a catalyst to build unity, bridge gaps, and catapult the organization forward. Organizations are able to improve and transform culture over time, meet challenges, and remain viable when their leaders understand the art of change.

In all organizations, there are "dragons" with unique talents, strengths, and behavior patterns that allow them to control their own territory. They tend to believe change is a threat and are therefore resistant to change. However, this resistance can be overcome as a dragon matures in leadership with the help of a dragon slayer.

DRAGON SLAYERS

Change results from leadership and requires
unfreezing the current state and creating
conditions for a new state to be successful.

Dragon slayers are change agents or leaders skilled at optimizing the unique characteristics and talents of dragons to create positive change. Their work is never easy, but it is very rewarding. Ultimately, they have the ability to guide dragons in becoming dragon slayers themselves.

The following pages tell a story that will open your eyes, mind, and heart to the unique and wonderful world of dragon slayer leadership. The story is meant to serve as a source of insight, understanding, and reflection about leading change. You may not know the individual characters in the story, but you may recognize someone in your organization that acts as they do. You may even see yourself in the dragons or dragon slayers. In any case, keep your eyes, mind, and heart open as the battle for change begins in the Valley of Good Enough.

The Valley of Good Enough

The air is wet with cool mist. There in the foreground is the road to change. It is poorly lit and lacks direction markers or signage. In fact, it is overgrown with thorny brush and rocky pavement. Still, it is clear the road needs to be braved in order to benefit the multitudes and move past this place of "good enough" and "always done it this way." Actually, the time for change is overdue. This particular road has been eyed for many years. It's commonly known that it leads to a new and promising place with a potential for transformation that could benefit those in this area of the world and perhaps worldwide.

Time is running out, and those living in the Valley of Good Enough will surely lose their ability to live in the comfort they have grown accustomed to if the road to the Land of Progress is not opened. The Land of Progress holds promise and opportunity for new technology, processes, and development. The thought of it is exciting, but everyone knows it will result in changes to the current culture and, ultimately, may mean a loss of what is familiar and customary. There are more than a handful of reasons for the delay in moving on the road to change. Mainly, the delay can be attributed to the dragons mulling about, each with his or her own self-righteous cause. It isn't as though they have orchestrated an organized set of barriers, but they are still powerful enough to deter progress and halt forward movement.

There has hardly been a reason for anyone to challenge the dragons. Though different from one another and frequently in competition with each other, they have gained expertise in hindering advancement toward change. It has reached the point that anyone with so much as a thought of leading them has retreated in fear, humiliation, or frustration. It is evident that a different approach is necessary if movement down the road to change is ever to be realized.

Dragons are tough. Most of them have been around for a long time. They have networks of allies, clever hiding places, and specialized skill sets that allow them to use their influence for control. Their power is in their well-defined tactics. The only way to counter a dragon is to commission a dragon slayer.

Dragon slayers have characteristics and competencies that make them the obvious choice for taking on dragons. They are able to not only identify a dragon, but they have an inherent gift for assessing the dragon's control tactic and influencing them so change can be accomplished.

Dragon slayers have spent enough time being blocked by dragons to learn their nature, tendencies, and unique characteristics. With that knowledge and insight, dragon slayers can effectively engage dragons. In the worst-case scenario, they use specialized techniques and weaponry they have mastered to slay the dragon—but winning over a dragon is the first and most important goal of dragon slayers.

The dragon slayer who undertakes the challenge of opening the road to change undoubtedly requires courage, tenacity, creativity, and a clear vision.

The King of Change has tried repeatedly to have the dragons from the Valley of Good Enough help clear the road to the Land of Progress, but he has never been successful. It is as though the dragons know every possible way to keep things just as they have been for years. They used their energy, power, and effort to do whatever was necessary to maintain the comfortable status quo. They believed change would surely threaten the life they had grown accustomed too. The truth of the matter is that without change, they will lose their ability to survive.

The King knew he had to take bold action to save the Valley of Good Enough. He needed to persuade the dragons to align and open up the road to the Land of Progress. The King recognized that he needed a skilled dragon slayer to lead the charge, so he appointed Passion.

DRAGON SLAYERS

Always seek wise counsel.

Passion has grown up in this environment and understands what is required. She is driven by prior successes and a compelling desire to bridge the gaps between the dragons and gain the momentum necessary to start on a journey to change.

Passion understands the enormous challenge before her and realizes she can't face the dragons alone. She thinks about what she needs to do. She wants to do what is best but worries about her ability to lead the dragons. She knows that she needs the counsel of a thought partner to plan a strategy, so she heads off to the quietest part of the land to seek out the Wizard of Opportunity. She has known the Wizard for many years and trusts her judgment. The Wizard is very logical and the most inspirational person Passion has ever met. The Wizard has a way of listening and knowing the exact advice to offer in difficult situations.

Passion fills the Wizard in on the situation. The Wizard listens and then sits back and smiles. "I know just what you need to do. You need to have the dragons become a team. Right now, they are each only interested in their own agenda. They are individually frozen in their current comfortable state. Your job is to have them move into a new state where they can work together for the benefit of everyone."

The Wizard also has advice for Passion about not taking on the challenge alone. She talks about the benefits of having others with various skill sets join together to solve tough problems. Passion is energized and gains much clarity from her visit to the Wizard. She knows what she needs to do to ensure she does not let the King of Change down.

Passion then solicits the assistance of two other dragon slayers, Valor and Wisdom, and her trusted long-time friend, Strength. Passion believes her chances of leading the dragons to change are far better with the partnership of these trusted individuals.

DRAGON SLAYERS

Never slay a dragon alone.

Valor possesses a pure and kind heart. He has the ability to tame the impatient and unbelieving by painting a vivid picture of the future with clear language and a calm disposition. He never tires and is more forward thinking than anyone else in the Valley of Good Enough. His desire to serve motivates him in the face of difficulty. He can see potential in any situation and always has his eyes on the future.

Wisdom is based in reality but keeps one foot in possibilities and dabbles in ingenuity. Her political sense is part of her DNA. She is critical at times, but always self-manages her emotions and is a no-nonsense leader. She is straightforward, driven, and possesses the gift of clarity.

Strength is grounded and unimpressed by conflict. She has nerves of steel and remains calm, cool, and collected even in the most tenuous circumstances. Although not yet a dragon slayer, she is, in fact, the force that supported Passion in becoming the successful dragon slayer she is.

Together, Passion, Valor, Wisdom, and Strength agree to partner on a mission to engage each dragon that stands in the way of opening up the road to the Land of Progress. With their mission in mind, they don their armor to slay dragons.

Their armor includes a dragon slayer helmet that provides serenity and clear thought. A breastplate guards their hearts physically and emotionally from negativity, unbelief, and distress. A belt surrounds their waists to remind them of the need to proceed in truth and nobility. They wear sturdy boots to maintain secure footing and steadiness on the path, even when they are tripped up by unsuspecting traps.

Each dragon slayer carries a shield to deflect the arrows of counterattack, which frequently present as fiery flames of anger and passive aggressiveness. Most important of all, they are each armed with a sword, which presents as words that are thoughtfully spoken to melt away doubt and fear.

DRAGON SLAYERS

Armor is important.

The first dragon they approach is Puff. Puff is the most boastful and proud dragon. He stands tall and confident in the face of every challenge. He has a way of twisting reality to benefit his own agenda. He is sly, smart, and knows enough about fire breathing to design and execute the perfect deterrent, often disguised as a leap of forward movement.

The dragon-slaying approach that works best with this type of puffed up dragon is to allow them to claim the change strategy as one they designed themselves. In fact, placing this dragon in a place of honor among all the other dragons will result in alignment and cooperation. He will, in essence, lead the charge right along with the dragon slayers.

Passion allows Valor to take the lead in approaching Puff. Valor has the ability to share the vision of change that is so desperately needed. He asks Puff for his insights and expertise in designing a solution for opening up the road to the Land of Progress. Valor and the other dragon slayers listen while Puff describes the way he would improve life in the Valley of Good Enough. He is really quite creative and logical when given the opportunity to solve a problem privately, away from the limelight of the other dragons.

Puff agrees to hold off on fire breathing long enough to share the idea for opening the road to the Land of Progress with the other dragons.

Passion thanks Puff. Wisdom assures him that his idea and willingness to help them will mean so much to so many. The Land of Progress offers the promise to provide resources they are lacking and open up the possibilities to provide services that are not available in the Valley of Good Enough. Strength arranges for the team to take a short trip to meet the next most important dragon, Iam Solo.

Iam Solo is a meek and kind-hearted dragon. He gets his power from developing progressive and award-winning ventures. He likes to bolster his reputation and enjoys having the other dragons rally around and support him when he wins an award. He actually enjoys new ideas as long as they are in his time and in his way. Winning him over requires skill to keep him from retreating into his own world of individual progress.

Wisdom asks Puff if he will share his ideas for change with Iam Solo. After Puff describes how opening the road to progress will make a huge difference, he asks Iam Solo if he knows a way to capitalize on the change effort to gain notoriety. Puff easily convinces Iam Solo that he will be famous in no time if he joins in the mission. Of course, Iam Solo cannot miss out on this once-in-a-lifetime opportunity and agrees to join in the change effort.

Passion knows that she and the dragon slayers are well on their way to implementing change in the Valley of Good Enough. She also knows that in order to continue to gain the momentum necessary for success, the dragon slayers will need to solicit the support of one of the most difficult and very outgoing dragons, Con Troller.

He is what most would consider a socialite, though others may call him a ringleader. He is very vocal and usually has something to say about everything. He likes change. Well, actually he likes to be a barrier to change. He finds an issue with just about everything and stops change in its tracks. He talks in circles and distract with ease those attempting to make change.

You can always tell when you encounter this kind of dragon by his inability to stop talking and start listening. He loves hearing himself talk and can take over most discussions with a twisted, voluminous array of stories.

DRAGON SLAYERS

Dragons stick together. If you can win over one dragon, your chance of others following will increase.

Passion knows that winning over Con Troller is important because Con Troller is a natural communicator. He will spread negative information across the land if he disagrees with the plan for change. However, if he is on board, he will be the dragon slayers' biggest promoter of the plan for change. As the dragon slayers approach the domain of Con Troller, they realize he is not alone. He has a visitor, Powerbul, whom he has mentored.

Powerbul is a smart and powerful bully. She has two heads and acts as though she is in charge, but she is really totally out of touch with all that is going on around her. She maintains authority and position by using clever words and tactics that cause others to believe she is an intellectual expert. She is clever and cunning, with an ability to maintain just enough contact to appear busy and important.

She is skilled at covering the truth while articulating her desire to be transparent. She appears calm and composed, especially when others in authority are around, but if you cross her, she resorts to emotional displays of anger and will destroy anything that gets in her way.

Powerbul has also learned a trait that her mentor Con Troller has mastered. They both have an obsession with being in charge, even when they are not supposed to be. They are masters at attempting to revise any strategy that has been developed by someone else so it reflects their own ideas. They also overcompensate when they feel out of control, and they have a tendency to micromanage.

The dragon slayers let Puff and Iam Solo begin the conversation about the need for change. They speak about change with great enthusiasm, as if it is something they've always wanted but could never achieve because of the King's incompetence. They reference the dragon slayers as though they are accomplices in what the two of them describe as "an obvious, much-needed plan for change."

Of course, Con Troller and Powerbul think they should go off and design a very complex change strategy and then get back together with the dragon slayers at a later date. Wisdom and Valor can hardly contain themselves. Wisdom notes there is a need to move forward quickly and that there is a sense of urgency to clear the road.

Valor creates a beautiful word picture of what the future will be like. He focuses on the benefits to the dragons and talks to them about the legacy they will leave for future generations if they just join them. He says that it will be impossible to move forward without them because they are so influential and respected.

Con Troller and Powerbul agree they can make a difference and provide just the guidance the dragon slayers need. They can see themselves as potentially having more credibility and power once the road opens up because of them. In fact, they think they will be able to move to the Land of Progress and become elected leaders if they play their cards right.

Strength does what she can to create a common set of documents to capture all the agreements reached between the dragons and the dragon slayers. She is amazed with the way the dragon slayers have gained the commitment of the dragons with very little difficulty. It seems almost too easy.

The next day Passion, Wisdom, and Valor travel to the opposite end of the land. There they meet with one of the most effective dragons, Elitist, an opinionated expert. Her environment, team, and strategy are impeccable. She knows she's the best dragon and the envy of all the land. She displays an air of superiority. This enables her to control her position and others, especially those with less-than-healthy dragon egos.

The dragon slayers inform her of their partnership with the other dragons. They share the plan to move forward for change and progress. They let Elitist know they are likely to discover something new in the Land of Progress to make the other dragons even more successful than she is.

DRAGON SLAYERS

Know your dragon. What works to slay one
dragon may not work to slay another.

Just the thought of that causes Elitist to be interested in what the dragon slayers have to say. She would never want to be left behind, is very competitive, and has a strong desire to be better than the others. The dragon slayers dislike Elitist's sense of superiority.

Even so, they think it will be better to have her on board because she possesses some great tools and processes. She agrees to join them but notes that she has very specific protocols for engagement. She must have her needs met in order to feel a part of the team.

Passion is very concerned about one other dragon that could be detrimental to the team. Heel Digger has been around a long time. She appears to collaborate and engage with others, but her entire strategic arsenal rests in her ability to dig in her heels. In doing so, she becomes immovable.

It is like encountering a mountain or a giant bolder. You think you can chip away at her tenacious exterior, but she is untouchable and will drain everyone of all energy while they try to drag her into change.

Passion is sure that Heel Digger will not be a good partner for the team. Valor feels that Heel Digger deserves a chance. Wisdom clarifies for Valor the concerns Passion has. She agrees with Passion and recognizes that Heel Digger will not only drain them of all their energy and momentum, she will also slow forward movement to virtually a standstill. This is a dragon they really need to have out of the way.

The dragon slayers all agree that Heel Digger will not be asked to join in the change process. If she decides to come along later on her own, that will be just fine. For now, though, they decide to not engage Heel Digger at all.

DRAGON SLAYERS

Don't waste your time and energy of
heel diggers.

The dragon slayers move on to meet Doitall, the mightiest of the dragons. He is fearless, proud, and diversified in his approach. There is nothing that escapes his grasp or sight. With everything within his reach, he can develop interventions the other dragons only dream about. His resources are varied, and this variety allows for long-term control. He really has no desire or need to change. He much prefers that others change to meet his needs and requirements.

Valor wonders what the dragon slayers can do to have Doitall join forces for change. It is obvious that the strategies used to mobilize the other dragons will not work in this situation. Passion worries that with Heel Digger left behind, it will be essential to convince Doitall to join them.

The dragon slayers know they need to have a critical mass of the dragons on board to make change a reality. Without Doitall, the chances of that happening are diminished.

Doitall hears the plea of the dragon slayers, but it sounds like he will need to give up too much to join the other dragons in clearing the road. He likes being different. It makes him feel powerful and, well, important. Wisdom can sense Doitall's need to feel important, but she realizes he is necessary to the change effort. She has an idea.

At Wisdom's request, Strength calls together the five dragons that have agreed to work toward change. Puff, Iam Solo, Con Troller, Powerbul, and Elitist are a bit apprehensive about what lies ahead. Still, they have given their word to the dragon slayers that they will do what they can to leave behind their own perspectives and join forces to utilize their skills to better the community.

The dragon slayers have a heart-to-heart talk with the dragons. There is discussion about how far they have already come in just agreeing to join forces and move toward the Land of Progress.

Wisdom shares her concern about needing as many of the dragons as possible to help to clear the road and begin the journey. They certainly need all the dragons' diverse strengths and powerful skills. Of course, they will benefit greatly if they can secure the support of Doitall. The only problem is that the dragon slayers do not have the ability to engage Doitall alone.

The Dragon Slayers realize they stand a greater chance of winning over Doitall if the dragons help convince him. After all, he is one of them! They are more influential and knowledgeable about dragon etiquette than the dragon slayers are. What if they could influence Doitall together—well, that is, if they are powerful enough. Of course, the dragons rise to the challenge. They head off to engage Doitall and persuade him to bring the very specialized, one-of-a-kind support they need. He surely will have a hard time turning down almost all the dragons in the land.

Doitall is impressed beyond words! He feels important and very powerful. He figures that no matter what happens once the road to change opens, he still possesses specialized and necessary things the dragons will need. It is a win/win situation for him to help the dragon slayers.

DRAGON SLAYERS

Critical mass is necessary for change to take place.

The Land of Progress

So off they go, the three dragon slayers, the six dragons, and right there beside them, Strength. Once they reach the road, Puff shoots out a plume of fire that virtually disintegrates all the brush that had blocked the way. Con Troller begins telling every living thing what has happened and a huge crowd forms.

Everyone is in total awe! Never before have the creatures of the Valley of Good Enough seen such a display of unity and conquest. Even Heel Digger comes roaming out of her corner of the valley to see what all the commotion is about.

There is an energy present that has never been displayed before. Elitist begins organizing the rubble and designing a path. Passion partners with Puff; Valor with Powerbul; and Wisdom with Doitall as they journey down the path designed by Elitist.

It is a long journey. Strength keeps track of where they are headed and makes sure everyone has what they need. At first, everyone is out of step and disorganized, but as they venture down the road to change they gain coordination and ease. Soon they reach the Land of Progress. It looks different than any of them had imagined. It is brighter, bigger, and has so much to offer.

Several dragon slayers from the Land of Progress approach them wearing very different armor with bright lights and sounds. They are surprised to see the dragons that Passion, Valor, and Wisdom brought along.

Apparently, the dragons that once lived in the Land of Progress have moved further west to the Land of Innovation, where they have all learned to fly. Fly? The dragons stand in amazement while they contemplate that. They have never heard of such a thing, but the thought of what is possible thrills them more than ever. Even Heel Digger finds herself dancing on her toes in delight.

The world and everything it has to offer has suddenly taken on a whole new meaning—and to think, this has always been available. If only they had opened the road to change sooner! The King of Change arrives just in time to see faces of pure joy on the dragons and the dragon slayers.

"Passion!" he calls. "You have pleased me with your dragon slaying skills and successful strategy to bring change to the Valley of Good Enough."

DRAGON SLAYERS

Leadership requires passion, valor, wisdom and strength, as well as a long-term commitment to stay faithful in the change effort.

Passion smiles and hugs Valor, Wisdom, and Strength in celebration. "I could have never done it alone. It took the entire team and the advice of a wise counselor to make it happen. Honestly, dragon slaying is easy when you listen with your heart and lead with your soul," she says.

The future is bright for the Valley of Good Enough. The King of Change begins conversations with the leaders of the Land of Progress and the Land of Innovation. Together, they discover a new world of possibilities to explore.

The opportunities are limitless, as is the newfound confidence of the team from the Valley of Good Enough, now enjoying the sights of a whole new land.

Dragon Slayer's Keys to Leading Change

1. Always seek wise counsel.

2. Never attempt to slay a dragon alone.

3. Know your dragon. What works to slay one dragon may not work for another.

4. Dragons stick together. If you can win over one dragon, your chance of others following will increase.

5. Armor is important:

   * Be sure you maintain a clear head.

   * Guard your heart from negativity, unbelief, and distress.

   * Proceed in truth and nobility.

   * Maintain secure footing and steadiness on the path, even when tripped up by hidden traps.

   * Shield yourself from fiery flames of anger and passive aggressiveness.

   • Use words that are thoughtfully spoken to melt away doubt and fear.

Dragon Slayer's Keys to Leading Change Continued

6. The road to change often seems dark and difficult to navigate, but once started it becomes easier.

7. Don't waste your time and energy on Heel Diggers.

8. Critical mass is necessary for change to take place.

9. Change results from leadership and requires unfreezing the current state and creating the conditions for a new state to be successful.

10. Leadership requires passion, valor, wisdom, and strength, as well as a long-term commitment to stay faithful in the change effort.

Dragon Slayer's Change Checklist

1. Change Sponsor

2. Desired Change Clearly Defined

3. Sense of Urgency

4. Indicators of success (how will you know change occurred)

5. Leader(s) with passion, wisdom, and valor

6. Strong project manager or organizer

7. Know your dragons (who are you trying to influence)

8. Wise counsel to design the plan

9. Implement the plan with frequent check-ins and redirection if needed

10. Communicate results and celebrate

Dragon Slayer Versus Dragon Qualities

Review the qualities noting whether an individual displays more Dragon Slayer or Dragon behaviors.

QUALITIES OF A DRAGON SLAYER

1. Supports need for change.
2. Has the best interest of those served at heart.
3. Has prior success and confidence.
4. Collaborates with others when appropriate.
5. Values the power of teamwork.
6. Seeks wise counsel in planning a strategy.
7. Desires to serve others.
8. Forward thinking with a clear vision for the future.
9. Politically astute.
10. Grounded and emotionally intelligent.

QUALITIES OF A DRAGON

1. Likes the status quo and "the way we always do things."

2. Has own best interest or that of own immediate territory at heart.

3. Overconfident or unaware of the way others perceive them.

4. Often exceeds scope or limits scope.

5. Values "I" or those in own immediate territory rather than organization at large.

6. Prefers to make decisions alone.

7. Self-serving.

8. Fails to consider future or sees future as opportunity to benefit self or immediate territory.

9. Uses political process for own gain.

10. Lacks emotional intelligence at times and may be called hot-headed, self-centered, uncooperative, or stubborn.

DRAGON SLAYERS

Change agent or leader skilled at optimizing the unique characteristics of individuals to create positive change. Requires courage, tenacity, creativity, and a clear vision.

Passion

* Intense, enthusiastic devotion to a cause.
* Tireless diligence, supernatural energy, and long-term commitment.
* Conviction to be a driving force.
* Has ability or gift for assessing the characteristics of individuals and influencing them so change can be accomplished.

Wisdom

* Deep understanding of people, events, or situations, resulting in the ability to apply perceptions and judgments.
* Based in reality but has one foot in the possibilities and dabbles in ingenuity.
* Has a political sense.
* May be critical at times, but always self-manages emotions.
* No-nonsense leader.
* Straightforward, driven, and possesses the gift of clarity.

Valor

* Ability to encounter danger with firmness and personal bravery.

* Determination, boldness, and heroic courage.

* Possesses a pure and kind heart.

* Has the ability for taming the impatient and unbelieving by painting a vivid picture of the future with clear language and a calm disposition.

* Never tires.

* More forward thinking than anyone else.

* Desire to serve.

* Sees potential in any situation and has eyes on the future.

Dragon Slayer Armor

Helmet: Protection, serenity, and clear thought.

Breastplate: Guard heart physically and emotionally from negativity, unbelief, and distress.

Belt: Reminder to proceed in truth and nobility.

Sturdy Boots: Maintain secure footing and steadiness on the path, even when tripped up by hidden traps

Shield: Deflect the arrows of counterattack, which are frequently presented not only as fiery flames of anger, but also as passive aggressiveness.

Sword: Words that are thoughtfully spoken to melt away doubt and fear.

DRAGONS

Believes change is a threat. Frequently use their energy, power, and effort to do whatever is necessary to maintain the status quo. Has network of allies, clever hiding places, and specialized skill sets that allow them to use their influence for control.

Puff (Dragon)

> * Boastful and proud.

> * Confident in the face of every challenge.

> * Twists reality to benefit own agenda.

> * Sly, smart, and able to execute the perfect deterrent, often disguised as a leap of forward movement.

Approach: Share the vision privately away from the limelight of the other dragons. Ask for insights and expertise in designing a solution. Allow them to claim the change strategy as one they designed themselves. Place them in a place of honor among others, and they will in essence lead the charge right along the leaders.

Iam Solo (Dragon)

* Meek and kind-hearted.

* Gets power from developing progressive, new, or award-winning ventures.

* Likes to bolster their reputation and enjoys having others rally around and acknowledge their success.

* Actually enjoys new ideas as long as they are in their time and way.

* May be passive aggressive, acting as though they are on board with change but actually doing their own thing.

Approach: Emphasize how they will achieve notoriety, public acknowledgement, awards or ability to publish/be famous if they are part of the change. Keep them at the center of the action and interacting with others to prevent them from retreating into their own world of individual progress.

Con Troller (Dragon)

* Socialite or ringleader.
* Very vocal and usually has something to say about everything.
* Likes being a change barrier.
* Will find an issue with just about everything and stop change in its tracks.
* Can talk in circles and easily distract those attempting to make change.
* Inability to stop talking and start listening.
* Loves hearing themselves talk and can take over most discussions with a twisted, voluminous array of stories.
* *Obsessed with being in charge even when they are not supposed to be.
* *Masterful at attempting to revise any strategy that has been developed by someone else to have it be reflective of their own ideas.
* *Will overcompensate when they feel out of control with a tendency to micromanage.

Note: May be the mentor to a less senior individual.

Approach: Focus on the benefits to the change, what it may mean for their future, and the legacy they will leave. Emphasize their influence is needed and how much they are respected. Remind them they are really knowledgeable and others need their expertise. Utilize them as natural communicator/promoter of the change.

Powerbul (Dragon)

* Smart and powerful.

* Acts as though in charge, but totally out of touch with all that is going on around them.

* Uses clever words that lead others to believe they are an intellectual expert.

* Cleaver and cunning, with an ability to maintain just enough contact to appear busy and important.

* Skilled at covering up the truth while articulating a desire to be transparent. If crossed, resorts to emotional displays of anger.

* Will destroy anyone in the way.

* See double starred items for Con Troller that apply here as well.

Note: Often does not act alone. May have been mentored by a more senior individual.

Approach: Same as Con Troller

Elitist (Dragon)

* An opinionated expert.

* Their environment, team, and strategy are impeccable.

* Knows they are the best and the envy of all the others.

* Displays an air of superiority.

* Has a strong competitive spirit and desire to be better than others.

Note: This dragon requires special handling to feel part of the team and may try to undermine efforts of the leader if not included.

Approach: Let them know that others are likely to be even more successful than they are if they don't join the change effort. They never want to be left behind.

Heel Digger (Dragon)

* Appears to collaborate and engage with others but is immovable.

* Tenacious exterior.

* Will drain everyone's energy and momentum.

* Like encountering a giant boulder or mountain.

* Refuses to change.

Approach: Keep out of the change process. They will either leave or come along later.

Doitall (Dragon)

* Fearless, proud, and diversified.

* Has access to varied, specialized or special resources.

* Can do and create what others only dream of.

* Sees no need to change.

Approach: Bring other dragons along for influence. Responds best when made to feel important, special, and needed.

DRAGON
SLAYER HEROES

The King of Change

* Has a vision for improvement and a sense of urgency.
* Knows his abilities and limitations.
* Sees the potential in others.
* Provides resources needed for change.
* Acknowledges success and those who accomplished it.

Strength

* Grounded.
* Unimpressed by conflict.
* Nerves of steel.
* Remains calm, cool, and collected even in the most tenuous circumstances.
* Stabilizing force in the midst of chaos.

Wizard of Opportunity

* Trusted advisor.
* Has good judgment.
* Very logical.
* Inspirational.
* Good listener.
* Understands the power of teamwork.

Drop By for a Visit to our Website at

www.dragonslayerleader.com